NBA Action from A to Z

by James Preller

SCHOLASTIC INC.

New York   Toronto   London   Auckland   Sydney

To Seth, whose photo research and enthusiasm
helped make this book such a pleasure to make. — J.P.

Photo Credits
Front Cover, 13, 30: NBA/Jeff Reinking. **Back Cover, 17, 23, 27:** NBA/Nathaniel S. Butler. **3, 4, 15, 22,
24:** NBA/Andrew D. Bernstein. **5:** NBA/Doug Devoe. **6:** NBA/Layne Murdock. **7:** NBA/Richard Lewis. **8:**
NBA/Sam Forencich. **10, 25:** NBA/Jerry Wachter. **12, 16, 32:** Noren Trotman. **14:** NBA/Gregg Forwerk.
20: NBA/Gary Dineen. **21:** NBA/Chris Covetta. **26:** NBA/Tim Defrisco. **28:** NBA/Bill Baptist. **29 (large
clipboard):** NBA/Bill Smith. **29 (team huddle):** NBA/Fernando Medina.

ISBN 0-590-13768-9

© 1997 by NBA Properties, Inc.
All rights reserved. Published by Scholastic Inc.

12 11 10   2/0

Printed in the U.S.A.
First Scholastic printing, February 1997
Book design: Gewirtz Graphics, Inc.

Action

Basketball is a great game, filled with nonstop action and excitement.

Michael Finley gets sandwiched between Vlade Divac and Elden Campbell. Action is the name of the game.

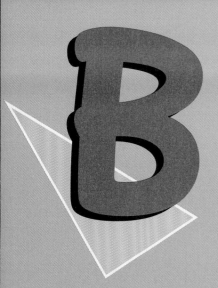

B

To play basketball, all you need is a hoop and a basketball.

Players have all sorts of funny nicknames for the basketball, like "pill," "rock," and "bean."

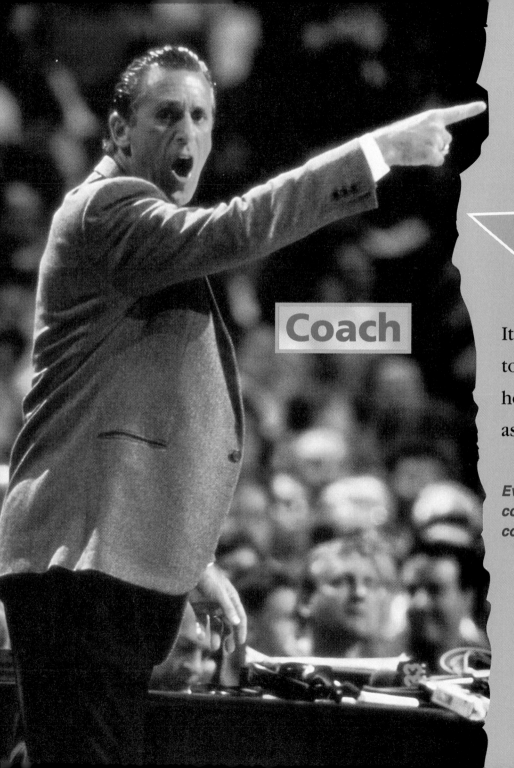

C

Coach

It is the coach's job to teach his players how to work together as a team.

Every NBA team has a coach. Pat Riley is the coach of the Miami Heat.

D

Dribbling—bouncing the basketball on the floor—is the most common way to move the ball up and down the court.

John Starks dribbles past Mitch Richmond.

E

Effort

It takes hard work and effort to become a great basketball player.

At only five feet three inches, Muggsy Bogues is the smallest player in NBA history.

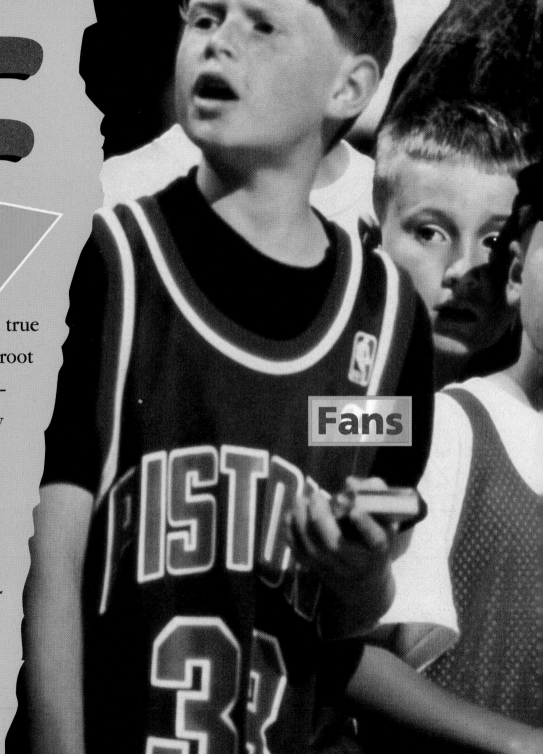

F

When you are a true fan, you always root for your team — even when they lose.

Being a fan makes basketball fun. It almost makes you feel like you are in the game with your favorite team.

Fans

Gorilla

G

Look! Up in the air!
It's a bird...
it's a plane...
it's a GORILLA?!

The Gorilla is a mascot for the Phoenix Suns. He often dazzles the crowd at halftime with high-flying dunks.

H

The first hoop was a peach basket nailed to a wall in 1891 by Dr. James Naismith, the inventor of basketball.

The official NBA hoop, or basket, stands 10 feet above the floor.

Impossible

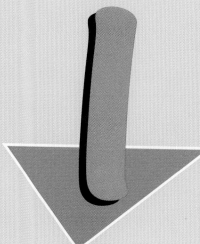

Every day in the NBA, players seem to do impossible things.

NBA players like Gary Payton can leap high, spin in the air, and make miraculous shots. Impossible? No, just incredible!

J

Jam

The slam dunk, or jam, is the most exciting play in basketball.

Hugo, a mascot for the Charlotte Hornets, goes up for a monster jam.

Kareem

Kareem Abdul-Jabbar scored more points than anyone in NBA history.

Kareem's favorite shot was called the Sky Hook.

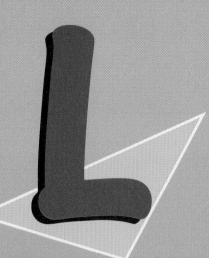

L

The layup is the easiest, surest shot in basketball.

Grant Hill glides in for a layup.

Layup

M

MVP stands for Most Valuable Player. It's a great honor to earn the MVP award.

Mitch Richmond was named MVP of the 1995 All-Star Game—and he's got the trophy to prove it!

NBA

The National Basketball Association includes 29 teams in the United States and Canada.

Each team has its own uniform, name, and logo. Which is your favorite?

Boston Celtics

Miami Heat

New Jersey Nets

Atlanta Hawks

Charlotte Hornets

Chicago Bulls

Dallas Mavericks

Denver Nuggets

Houston Rockets

Golden State Warriors

Los Angeles Clippers

Los Angeles Lakers

New York Knicks

Orlando Magic

Philadelphia 76ers

Washington Bullets

Cleveland Cavaliers

Detroit Pistons

Indiana Pacers

Milwaukee Bucks

Toronto Raptors

Minnesota Timberwolves

San Antonio Spurs

Utah Jazz

Vancouver Grizzlies

Phoenix Suns

Portland Trail Blazers

Sacramento Kings

Seattle Sonics

O

When a team has the ball, it is on offense. The team without the ball is on defense.

Sherman Douglas knows that when a team is on offense, it has one job: to score points!

Offense

Pass

Good players pass the ball to their team-mates, hoping to find an easy shot.

John Stockton is one of the best passers in the NBA.

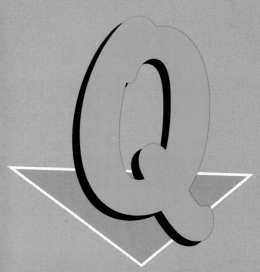

Q

Many smaller players use their quickness to beat bigger, stronger opponents.

Like a flash, little Spud Webb darts to the basket.

Quick

Referee

It's the referee's job to make sure that every game is played by the rules.

A referee calls a foul during a game.

Sneaker

Every player in the NBA wears sneakers to help him run faster and jump higher.

Shaquille O'Neal wears the largest sneakers in the NBA — size 22 EEE. That's 15½ inches long!

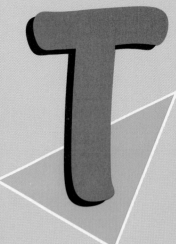

Most basketball players are very, very tall. The average height of a player in the NBA is six feet seven inches.

At seven feet seven inches, Gheorghe Muresan is one of the tallest men to ever play in the NBA.

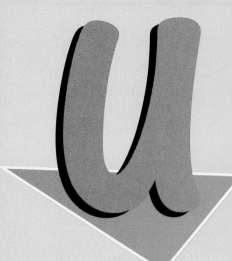

Fans can recognize their favorite teams by the familiar colors and designs of the uniforms.

Many fans like to wear the jerseys of their favorite players. This one is a little too big.

Uniform

V

When a player jumps high, fans often say he is "going vertical."

Many basketball players, like Dee Brown, are fantastic jumpers. They go vertical all the time!

Vertical

W

Every player dreams of winning an NBA championship. It means that your team is the best in the NBA.

Robert Horry holds the championship trophy. He won two championships with the Houston Rockets, in 1994 and 1995.

Win

A coach draws X's and O's to show his players where to stand and where to run.

Coach Phil Jackson teaches his team how to run a play. The X's stand for his players, while the O's represent the players on the opposing team.

X's and O's

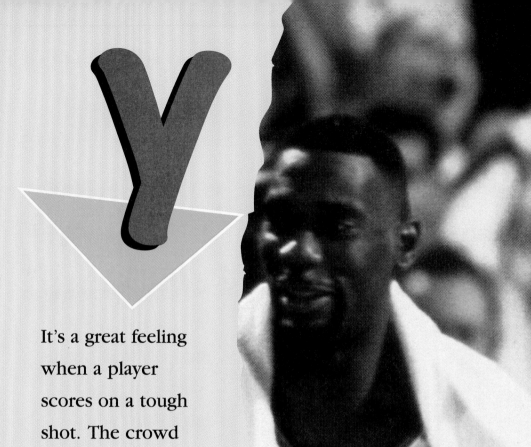

Y

"Yes!"

It's a great feeling when a player scores on a tough shot. The crowd cheers. The arena announcer roars, "Yes!"

Even if a player isn't in the game, he can help his team by cheering a great play.

Z

"Zo!"

Alonzo Mourning is an enthusiastic player. His friends and teammates call him "Zo."

Alonzo Mourning plays center for the Miami Heat.